# Hide and Seek

Grateful acknowledgement is made to:
Doug Allan: page 9 (bottom),
G. I. Bernard pages 5 (bottom), 13 (top), 17 (top left), 18 (top), 20,27,29 and cover
Derek Bromhall: page 23 (top)
Waina Cheng: page 19 (top)
Dr. J. A. L. Cooke: pages 12, 16, 18 (bottom), 23 (bottom), 28
Michael Fogden: pages 7 (top), 13 (bottom), 17 (bottom), 21 (bottom)
Philip Goddard: page 17 (top right)
Laurence Gould: page 26 (top)
Gareth Jones: page 5 (top)
Alison Kuiter: page 26 (bottom)
Rudie H. Kuiter: page 24
Mantis Wildlife Films/Oxford Scientific Films: page 22
Carsten Olesen/FOCI/OSF: page 9 (top)
Peter Parks: pages 14, 15, 25 (bottom)
Keith Porter: page 4
David Shale: page 25 (top)
D. H. Thompson: page 10
P & W Ward: pages 7 (bottom), 19 (bottom), 21 (top)
S. J. R. Woodell: page 6
Acknowledgement is also made to Survival Anglia for photographs by Jen and Des
Bartlett on page 11, by Joel Bennett on page 8 and by Dieter and Mary Plage on the
title page
Thanks are due to Sarah Cunliffe for research.

11.95    8786531

First American edition, 1986.
Originated and published in Great Britain by
Andre Deutsch Limited, 1986.
Printed and bound by Proost, Turnhout, Belgium
Library of Congress Cataloging-in-Publication Data
Hide and seek.
    Summary: Text and photographs present animals which
have permanent or intermittent camouflage capabilities
which aid in both preying and protecting.
    1. Camouflage (Biology) — Juvenile literature.
[1. Camouflage (Biology)]  I. Oxford Scientific Films.
QL767.H53  1986  591.57'2      86-560
ISBN 0-399-21342-2
G. P. Putnam's Sons, 51 Madison Avenue,
New York, New York 10010
First Impression

## Leopard

# Hide and Seek

**Oxford Scientific Films**

edited by

JENNIFER COLDREY and KAREN GOLDIE-MORRISON

G. P. Putnam's Sons, New York

# IN THE GRASS

Young grass is fresh and green. Older grass becomes dry and brown. Animals that hide in grass are usually green or brown, but sometimes striped or spotted.

**Meadow Grasshopper.** This grasshopper has a long, thin, green and brown body which matches the leaves and stems around it.

**Cheetah.** The cheetah is a fierce hunter. Its tawny spotted coat hides it well as it crouches in the long grass, on the lookout for prey, maybe an impala or a gazelle.

**Harvest Mouse and nest.** The tiny harvest mouse builds its nest of woven grass among the corn stalks. As the corn ripens and the grass turns brown, the harvest mouse and its nest of babies are hard to see.

# ON THE GROUND

Bare ground can be sandy, grey or patchy brown, and so are many of the animals that live there.

**Little Tern chick and eggs.** The speckled eggs and newly hatched chick of this Little Tern blend in well with the sand and pebbles on the beach.

**Texas Horned Lizard.** In the desert, birds of prey and other enemies find this lizard hard to spot against the sand.

**Gerbil.** The golden brown of this gerbil's coat matches the color of the sand in the African desert where it lives.

# IN THE SNOW

Animals that live in cold and snowy places are usually white, which makes them hard to see against a landscape of snow and ice.

**Polar Bear.** This large animal has few enemies. Its white coat disguises it well as it pads silently across the snow hunting for seals.

**Arctic Fox.** Here is another hunter of the far north. Its thick white fur is a good disguise in the snow.

**Snow Petrels.** These birds live near the South Pole. Their snow-white bodies are difficult to see as they crouch in the snow.

# IN THE TREES

Woodland colors are green and brown, with many spots of light and shade. Animals hiding in the trees are various shades of green and brown.

**Iguana Lizard.** A large green lizard lies in the sun in this tropical forest. From a distance it looks like part of the branch to which it clings.

**Tawny Frogmouths.**
Can you spot the two birds among the streaky brown branches of this tree?

# ON THE BARK

The bark of a tree is often rough and cracked. It may also have moss and other plants growing on it. Many animals hiding on tree trunks have mottled green and brown bodies which match the bark exactly.

**Huntsman Spider.** Spiders are common on tree trunks, and are difficult to see when they are not moving. Can you spot this one easily?

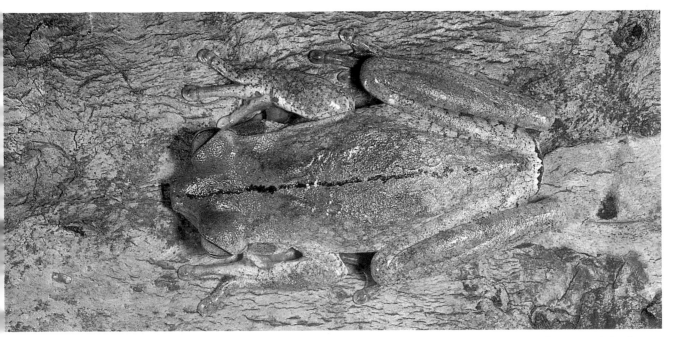

**Tree Frog.** A bird or snake will find it hard to spot this brown frog with its body flattened against the bark.

**Eyelash Viper.**
The scaly, mottled skin of this snake looks exactly like the rough, mossy bark of the tree.

# ON TOWN OR COUNTRY BARK

Many moths have spotted patterns on their wings and bodies. They are well hidden from the eyes of hungry birds when they rest on tree trunks during the day, but are only really safe when the bark matches their own colors.

**Peppered Moth on a tree in the country.** This speckled black and white moth is almost invisible as it rests on a tree trunk covered in lichens.

**Peppered Moth on a tree in town.** The same moth now lands on a tree trunk with dirty, black bark. It's easy to see how a bird could spot the moth here.

**Black Peppered Moth on a tree in town.** This black moth matches the sooty bark of a city tree.

# LIKE TWIGS OR THORNS

Some insects look like twigs or thorns. During the day they stay completely still and sharp-eyed enemies, such as birds or lizards, only notice them if they move.

**Pupa of Swallowtail Butterfly.** Can you believe that the short broken twig sticking out from this tree trunk is really the chrysalis of a butterfly? What clues give it away?

**Stick Insect.** Every part of this stick insect's body, including its legs and feelers, is long, thin and twig-like.

**Twig Caterpillar.** Can you spot the caterpillar on this twig?

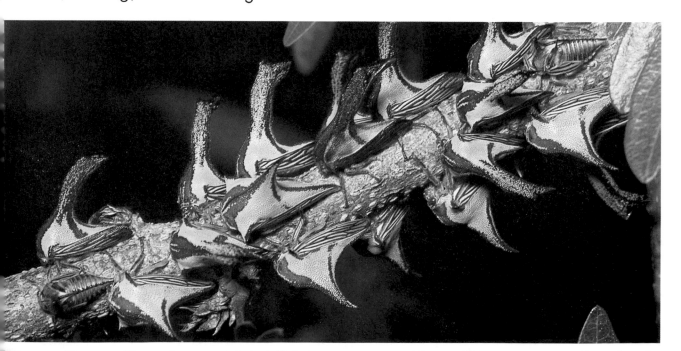

**Thorn Bugs.** To a hungry bird this may seem like a thorny stem. But look closely and you will see that it is really a mass of spiny insects.

17

# AMONG LIVING LEAVES

Many insects are not noticed by their enemies because they look like living leaves. Some even make strange movements that resemble a leaf trembling in the breeze.

**Leaf Hopper.** Can you spot the insect among these green leaves? What gives it away?

**Leaf-like Tree Hopper.** If you look closely, you can just make out this insect's eye and legs.

**Leaf-like Bush Cricket.** This cricket is a perfect copy of a leaf. The pale spots look like patches of mold which are often found on real leaves.

**Caterpillar of the Alder Moth.** This looks like a bird's dropping, but is it?

# AMONG DEAD LEAVES

Some animals look exactly like dead leaves. During the day, they escape from their enemies by keeping still and quiet.

**Silkmoth.** This brown, crinkled leaf is really the wings of a silkmoth resting on the ground.

**Leaf-fish.**
These dead leaves
have fallen into the
water. But one of
them is not a leaf.
Can you see which?

**Horned Frog.** A hungry snake will find it hard to spot this frog against the dead brown leaves on the forest floor.

# AMONG FLOWERS
Some insects and spiders fool their enemies by looking like flowers.

**Flower Mantis.**
A butterfly or bee will get a nasty shock when it visits this flower. Can you see why?

**Crab Spider on Dog Rose.**
The pale colors of this spider hide it as it waits to catch insects that visit the flower. Its disguise also protects it from other enemies such as birds.

**Flower Moth.**
Can you tell which is the moth and which is the flower?

# IN THE SEA

Animals living in the sea have many ways of escaping from their enemies. One of the best ways is to look like seaweed.

**Leafy Sea Dragon.** This clump of seaweed is actually a fish.

**Sargassum Angler Fish.** Can you see two strange-looking fishes among this mass of seaweed?

**Sargassum Crab.**
A small pale crab is hiding among this clump of seaweed. Can you spot it?

# ON THE SEA BED

Much of the sea bed is stony, sandy, muddy or rocky. The rocks may be covered in seaweed or coral. Animals hiding on the bottom of the sea must look like sand, stones, coral or seaweed.

**Scorpion Fish.**
Can you see a fish lurking in the seaweed and coral in this picture? Look for an eye, a mouth and a fin.

**Southern Octopus.**
This octopus is changing color so that its body will match the stony sea bed.

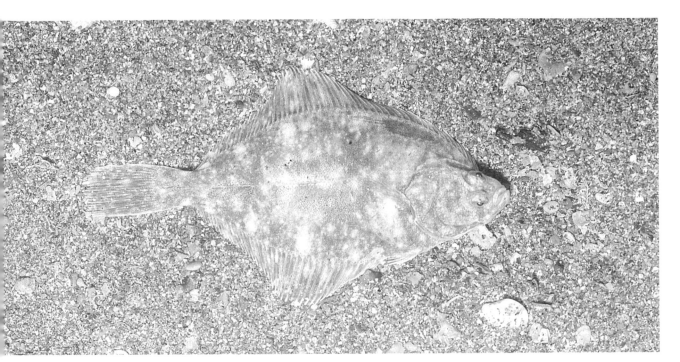

**Flounder.** A flounder can change the color of its skin to match the sea bottom. Here its flat, speckled body blends in well with the gravelly bottom.

Now it is lying on larger stones and shells. The patterns on its body are changing to match the background.

# WEARING A DISGUISE

One clever way of hiding from enemies is to wear a disguise. Some animals stick bits and pieces of things onto their bodies. This disguises them and sometimes protects them from attack.

**Spiny Spider Crab.** Can you see the crab under this wonderful coat of pink, red and green seaweed?

**Caddis Fly Larva.**
If you were a fish,
would you want to
eat this mass of
empty shells? It is
actually a caddis
fly larva in
disguise.

# MORE FACTS

## IN THE GRASS (pages 4-5)

**Meadow Grasshopper.** In spite of their singing, grasshoppers manage to hide themselves from birds and lizards by choosing a background to match their green and brown coloring.

**Cheetah.** The cheetah hunts small antelope (Impala and Gazelle) on the African plains. It will also attack hares and birds. It needs to be hidden from its prey as it creeps nearer, before making the final high speed dash for a kill.

**Harvest Mouse.** Harvest mice are active by day and spend a lot of time climbing in grass and corn. Their camouflage helps to protect them from ground-living enemies such as rats, weasels and foxes, and birds of prey from the air.

## ON THE GROUND (pages 6-7)

**Little Tern.** The nest is little more than a shallow indentation, with no nesting material to give it away. When the parents are away from the nest, the helpless chicks press close to the ground and are hidden from predators such as gulls, hawks and foxes.

**Texas Horned Lizard.** The mottled markings and spiny, tattered edges of the lizard break up its outline against the ground. The line down the back divides the body into two as a further distraction. When threatened, the lizard holds its flattened body close to the ground, which hides its shadow in the bright desert sunlight.

**Gerbil.** The colors of this desert gerbil help to hide it from predators such as foxes, jackals and birds of prey. Like many animals, the pale undersides lessen the shadow and make the outline of the body harder to see against a background of similar color. This is called *countershading*.

## IN THE SNOW (pages 8-9)

**Polar Bear.** Polar bears live in the North Polar region. They feed mainly on seals which they catch by creeping stealthily across the ice or by swimming around ice floes.

**Arctic Fox.** Only in winter do these animals have a white coat. In summer, when the snow south of the pole melts and landscape colors turn to greys and browns, the fox's coat also changes to a greyish-brown. Its disguise enables it to creep up on prey such as hares, lemmings and sea birds. It is also protection against its own enemies, such as timber wolves.

**Snow Petrels.** These birds nest and lay their o[ne] white egg in cracks or niches in the rocks. Th[e] white bodies protect them from enemies such [as] skuas (gull-like predators). They dive for fish a[nd] other creatures in the cold Antarctic sea, whe[re] their whiteness makes them invisible to unsu[s]pecting prey below.

## IN THE TREES (pages 10-11)

**Iguana Lizard.** Lizards need to bask in the sun [to] warm up their bodies so that they have enoug[h] energy to move and feed. Being green is [an] advantage for disguise in a tropical forest whe[re] the warm, moist atmosphere encourages lus[h] green growth on the tree trunks.

**Tawny Frogmouths.** These birds are a kind [of] nightjar or whippoorwill found in Australia. Durin[g] the day they rest in trees where they look exact[ly] like broken branches. Their large eyes are part[ly] closed but they peep through a chink to watch o[ut] for enemies.

## ON THE BARK (pages 12-13)

**Huntsman Spider.** The dark and light patterns [of] this large Australian spider (4″ across) help [to] disguise its body so that it looks like part of th[e] bark. It is often found on dead trees where [it] feeds on grubs and insects living in the bark.

**Tree Frog.** Tree frogs make tasty meals for man[y] predators. They are mainly active at night, b[ut] stay still, relying on camouflage, during the da[y.] They can change color quite rapidly to tone [in] with their surroundings.

**Eyelash Viper.** This snake feeds on frog[s,] lizards and small rodents, which it kills with i[ts] long poisonous fangs. Although it hunts mainly [at] night, its wonderful camouflage conceals it fro[m] other animals in the South American jungle. [It] often dangles from trees, clinging by its tail, an[d] looking like a hanging creeper or vine.

## ON TOWN OR COUNTRY BARK (pages 14-15)

**Peppered Moth.** These photographs all show th[e] same species. The speckled form has alwa[ys] been more common in rural areas of Britain an[d] Europe, where the air is clean and the trees a[re] covered with lichens. It is well camouflaged her[e.] The black form is rare in country areas where it [is] soon spotted by birds. During the last centur[y] the black form became more common aroun[d] towns and cities, where pollution from indust[ry] killed the lichens on the trees and blackened the[ir] trunks. The black moth survived in the tow[ns] while the speckled form, no longer camouflage[d,] began to die out there.

## KE TWIGS OR THORNS (pages 16-17)

**upa of Swallowtail Butterfly.** The fine girdle of
k and the banded segments at the lower end of
e body show that this apparent broken twig is
e pupa or chrysalis of a butterfly. The pale
een patches on the pupal skin exactly match
e lichens on the tree trunk. The pupa is a
lnerable stage in the life cycle of a butterfly
nce it cannot move to escape from enemies.

**ick Insect.** These marvelous twig mimics are
ainly tropical insects, related to grasshoppers,
it usually wingless. When at rest, the first pair
legs and antennae are drawn forward, the third
ir of legs held back, to make a stick-like pose.
ey can stay motionless for hours.

**wig Caterpillar.** The pink and green caterpillar
ands out stiffly from this birch twig, opposite the
id which is bursting into leaf. It clings to the
ig with its back legs only. During the winter this
iterpillar is brown to match the twigs on which it
bernates, but in spring it turns greenish-brown,
th pink lumps to imitate the buds before they
en.

**orn Bugs.** Can you spot the legs and red eyes
these insects? Each bug has a long spine
icking out from its body. They line up on stems
d creepers in the jungle where they stay still
d feed by piercing through to the plant's sap.

## MONG LIVING LEAVES (pages 18-19)

**af Hopper.** Once you have spotted the red
ie, you will see the bug among these leaves.
it a bird or lizard is unlikely to find it. Leaf hop-
rs, unlike most other insects, can sit and feed
thout moving at all. Their mouthparts pierce
to leaves and stems and suck out the sap.

**af-like Tree Hopper.** The body of this tropical
ig from Trinidad resembles a flat, greenish-
llow leaf with torn brown edges. The eyes and
gs are pale and inconspicuous, which helps to
sguise it even more.

**af-like Bush Cricket.** Not only is the shape
d color of this tropical insect exactly like a leaf;
also has leaf-like veins on its wing-cases and
arkings which resemble fungal decay or insect
mage. Bush crickets chew away at the leaves
night, when they cannot be seen.

**aterpillar of the Alder Moth.** With its body
isted round, the shiny appearance and large
hite patches on the skin make this caterpillar
ok exactly like a fresh bird dropping. The lumpy
obs along its back resemble the small seeds
iich birds often eat. Unless it moves, a bird is
likely to come down and investigate it.

## AMONG DEAD LEAVES (pages 20-21)

**Silkmoth.** Most moths are active at night when
they cannot be seen. During the day they stay
still and hide from their enemies. Notice the
curled and tattered edges of the wings on this
moth, and the line-markings which imitate leaf
veins.

**Leaf-fish.** This orange leaf-fish is lying on its
side in the shallow water of a mangrove swamp.
Its shape is exactly like a leaf because the tail is
transparent and can't be seen. The dark line
across its head disguises the eye, making it hard
for predators such as herons, egrets and terns to
spot.

**Horned Frog.** The patchy marks and blotches on
this tropical frog imitate the spots of mold and
decay on a dead leaf. The eye is cleverly hidden
within a dark patch of skin which looks like a
shadow beneath the upper surface of a leaf. The
horns stick out like the edges of a leaf.

## AMONG FLOWERS (pages 22-23)

**Flower Mantis** (Borneo). This delicate white
orchid is really a fierce young insect-eating
mantid with petal-like legs and body. To fool its
prey, it pretends to be a flower and waits,
motionless, to seize with its powerful front legs
any insect that comes too near. Some mantids
are large and colorful; and they often sit in
flowers that match their colors.

**Crab Spider.** Crab spiders do not spin webs to
catch their prey. Instead they lie in ambush, often
in flowers, waiting to pounce on bees, butterflies
or hoverflies which come to feed on nectar or
pollen. This spider's white body blends perfectly
with the center of the rose, and the brown spots
on its abdomen look like stamens. It can change
to pale green or yellow to match flowers of those
colors.

**Flower Moth.** You can pick out this moth found in
Trinidad by its two front legs which are clinging
onto the leaf. If you look closely you can see its
feathery antennae. The drooping pink wings of
this resting moth are similar to the petals of the
flower next to it. A bird or lizard would find it hard
to spot the difference.

## IN THE SEA (pages 24-25)

**Leafy Sea Dragon.** The remarkable camouflage of this Australian pipe-fish enables it to drift like seaweed through the water, where it feeds on tiny crustacea and small fish by sucking them up through its long snout. The disguise also helps it to escape from large predatory fish.

**Sargassum Angler Fish.** These grown fish and one baby live in the floating seaweed found in the Sargasso Sea. They feed on other animals in the weed such as shrimps, crabs and baby fish, etc. and lure their prey by waggling the spiny fin on top of the head. The color and patterns on the adult fish, together with its tattered pieces of skin, mimic the weed around it perfectly.

**Sargassum Crab.** Another member of the Sargassum community is this tiny 1" crab. Its legs are a different color from its body which helps to disguise its true form. It is difficult for hungry fishes swimming below or seabirds flying overhead to see the crab in the floating seaweed.

## ON THE SEA BED (pages 26-27)

**Scorpion Fish.** These fish live mainly in shallow, warm coastal waters. They rarely move but wait for small fish or other prey to swim near, then lunge forward rapidly, opening their mouths to suck in their prey.

**Southern Octopus.** Octopuses can change color and even the texture of their skin quickly to blend with any background. They are usually found in shallow water where they crawl around on the sea bed searching for crabs, their chief prey. They hunt at night and hide during the day.

**Flounder.** Like other flatfish, the flounder lives on the sea bottom. Its sensitive vision picks up the slightest changes in background color, and the skin on its back tones in accordingly. The underside of the flounder stays white. It becomes almost invisible as its flat body blends with the sand or stones. Flatfish sometimes cover their bodies with sand and even bury themselves completely, leaving only their eyes poking out. Predators like seals find them hard to spot.

## WEARING A DISGUISE (pages 28-29)

**Spiny Spider Crab.** Only the crab's legs can seen beneath its disguise. The hard outer shell covered with spines on which the crab h speared many different kinds of seaweed. It pic up the weed in its pincers, often tearing it in smaller pieces, before planting them on its she If it moves to a different place, it may change disguise by placing shells or gravel on its body match the new background.

**Caddis Fly Larva.** Young caddis flies live unde water in ponds and streams, where they may eaten by fishes, frogs and other predators. Th make a protective case from shells (others u sand, gravel or pieces of leaf and stem) whi they cement together with silk from their mouth